Guitar

Easy Concert Pieces
Leichte Konzertstücke

for Guitar
für Gitarre

Volume 3 / Band 3

Edited by / Herausgegeben von
Peter Ansorge
and / und Bruno Szordikowski

ED 22558
ISMN 979-0-001-16096-4

Volume 1 / Band 1
ED 21636

Volume 2 / Band 2
ED 21637

Cover illustration:
Light cone: © PROBilder – Fotolia.com

www.schott-music.com

Mainz · London · Berlin · Madrid · New York · Paris · Prague · Tokyo · Toronto
© 2016 SCHOTT MUSIC GmbH & Co. KG, Mainz · Printed in Germany

Impressum
CD:
Martin Hegel, Guitar
Recording: Peter Finger, Acoustic Music Studio, Osnabrück
© 2016 Schott Music GmbH & Co. KG, Mainz
Printed in Germany · BSS 57586

Preface

Choosing appropriate pieces of music is particularly important for your first performances on the concert platform. This third book of Easy Concert Pieces brings together pieces that can be performed to good effect after about three years of tuition. Alongside many familiar favourites are less well-known gems and arrangements of popular works from the piano repertoire, too. The pieces in this collection trace a journey through five centuries of guitar and lute music from John Dowland to Francis Poulenc. This book represents an ideal complement to almost any guitar tutorial method and a compendium of pieces for concerts and competitions. The CD recorded by Martin Hegel for practice at home provides encouragement for young musicians.

Peter Ansorge / Bruno Szordikowski
Translation Julia Rushworth

Vorwort

Bei den ersten Schritten auf der Bühne kommt der Auswahl geeigneter Spielliteratur eine besondere Bedeutung zu. Der 3. Band der Easy Concert Pieces versammelt wirkungsvolle Vortragsstücke, die nach etwa 3 Jahren Unterricht spielbar sind. Neben vielen Unterrichtsklassikern sind auch weniger bekannte Kleinode und Arrangements beliebter Werke der Klavierliteratur enthalten. Die Sammlung ist zugleich eine Reise durch 5 Jahrhunderte Gitarren- und Lautengeschichte von John Dowland bis zu Francis Poulenc. Das Heft ist eine ideale Ergänzung zu nahezu jedem Gitarrenlehrwerk und zugleich ein Kompendium für Konzerte und Wettbewerbe. Die von Martin Hegel eingespielte CD unterstützt die jungen Musiker/-innen beim häuslichen Üben.

Peter Ansorge / Bruno Szordikowski

Contents / Inhalt

Tuning notes / Stimmtöne (a = 440 Hz)

Branle Anglaise

Emanuel Adriaenssen
(1550–1604)
Arr.: Peter Ansorge / Bruno Szordikowski

Danse Anglaise

Anonymus
Arr.: Peter Ansorge / Bruno Szordikowski

Calleno custure me

Anonymus
(William Ballet's Lutebook)
Arr.: Peter Ansorge / Bruno Szordikowski

Villanico

Cesare Negri
(1535–1604)
Arr.: Peter Ansorge / Bruno Szordikowski

Welscher Tanz

Anonymus
(16th century)
Arr.: Peter Ansorge / Bruno Szordikowski

Wilson's Wilde

Anonymus
Arr.: Peter Ansorge / Bruno Szordikowski

Packington's Pound

Anonymus
Arr.: Peter Ansorge / Bruno Szordikowski

The Sick Tune

John Dowland
(1563–1626)
Arr.: Peter Ansorge / Bruno Szordikowski

My Lord Willoughby's Welcome Home

John Dowland
(1563–1626)
Arr.: Peter Ansorge / Bruno Szordikowski

Canarie
(mit Hupfauf)

Joachim van der Hove
(ca. 1567–1620)

Arr.: Peter Ansorge / Bruno Szordikowski

Sarabande

Anonymus
(Baltic Lute Book / Baltisches Lautenbuch, 1740)
Arr.: Peter Ansorge / Bruno Szordikowski

Aria

Anonymus
(Aussee Guitar Tabulature /
Ausseer Gitarrentabulatur, 18th century)
Arr.: Peter Ansorge / Bruno Szordikowski

Menuet

Robert de Visée
(1660–1720)
Arr.: Peter Ansorge / Bruno Szordikowski

Españoleta

Gaspar Sanz
(1640–1710)
Arr.: Peter Ansorge / Bruno Szordikowski

Echo

Valentin Hausmann
(ca. 1560–1614)
Arr.: Peter Ansorge / Bruno Szordikowski

Contradanza

Fernando Ferandière
(ca. 1740–1816)

Arr.: Peter Ansorge / Bruno Szordikowski

Allegro

a tempo

Cotillon

Jean Hotteterre
(1677–1720)
Arr.: Peter Ansorge / Bruno Szordikowski

Menuet

Johann Sebastian Bach
(1685–1750)
Arr.: Peter Ansorge / Bruno Szordikowski

Aria

Giuseppe Antonio Brescianello
(ca. 1690–1758)
Arr.: Peter Ansorge / Bruno Szordikowski

Grazioso

Mauro Giuliani
(1781–1829)

from / aus: Le Papillon op. 50 (No. 23)

Menuet

Dionisio Aguado
(1784–1849)

Romance / Romanze

Francesco Molino
(1768–1847)

Sicilienne

Ferdinando Carulli
(1770–1841)

Allegretto

Mauro Giuliani
(1871–1829)

*) Original:

from /aus: Le Papillon op. 50 (No. 5)

Pastorale

Matteo Carcassi
(1792–1853)

from / aus: Les récréations des commançans op. 21 (No. 16)

This page is left blank to save an unnecessary page turn.
Diese Seite bleibt aus wendetechnischen Gründen frei.

Study / Etüde

Fernando Sor
(1778–1839)

from / aus: 24 leçons progressives op. 31 (No. 6)

Andante

Johann Kaspar Mertz
(1806–1856)

Andante cantabile

Anton Diabelli
(1781–1858)

from / aus: 30 Very Easy Exercises / 30 sehr leichte Übungsstücke op. 39 (No. 11)

Andante grazioso

Wolfgang Amadeus Mozart
(1756–1791)
Arr.: Peter Ansorge / Bruno Szordikowski

from / aus: Sonata KV 331

This page is left blank to save an unnecessary page turn.
Diese Seite bleibt aus wendetechnischen Gründen frei.

Bagatelle

Heinrich Marschner
(1795–1861)
Arr.: Peter Ansorge / Bruno Szordikowski

*) Original:

from / aus: 12 Bagatelles op. 4 (No. 1)

Minore

D.C. al Fine

*) Original:

Waltz / Walzer

Anonymus
(ca. 1870)

Fine

Trio

D.C. al Fine

Little Piece / Stückchen

Robert Schumann
(1810–1856)
Arr.: Peter Ansorge / Bruno Szordikowski

*) Original:

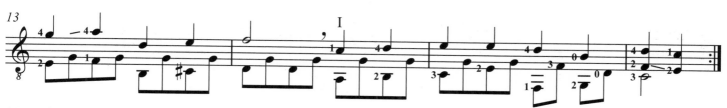

from / aus: Album for the Young / Album für die Jugend, op. 68 (No. 5)

Prélude

Frédéric Chopin
(1810–1849)
Arr.: Peter Ansorge / Bruno Szordikowski

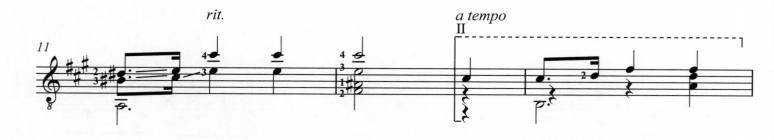

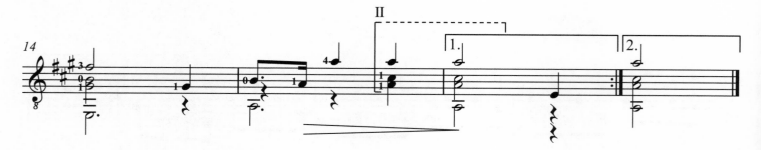

from / aus: 24 Préludes op. 28 (No. 7)

El testament d'Amelia

Katalanisches Volkslied

Arr.: Peter Ansorge / Bruno Szordikowski

Romanza

Anonymus
Arr.: Peter Ansorge / Bruno Szordikowski

Tiempo de vals

Julio Sagregas
(1879–1942)

Vals

Francisco Cimadevilla
(1861–1931)

from / aus: Tres piezas faciles y progresivas

Guagirana

Jacques Bosch
(1825–1895)

from / aus: 6 pièces faciles op. 89 (No. 2)

Mazurka

José Ferrer
(1835–1916)

Fine

D.C. al Fine

à Ida Presti

Sarabande

Francis Poulenc
(1899–1963)

Molto calmo e melanconico

Schott Music, Mainz 57 586